THAT'S AMAZING!

Welcome aboard!

Hello. I'm Ray Galactica and I'd like to welcome you to this amazing issue of *The Navigator*, which contains lots of fascinating facts and interesting information to get your brain cells buzzing. I'll introduce you to some fellow space-travellers who have learned to live and work in space. You'll also get the chance to see some extraordinary eclipses. Back down on Earth, your mission will be to accompany our secret agent on his travels. If you're feeling tired after all that, read our report about why you need sleep to live. No snoring, please!

Over and out!

Text Type	Literacy Skills	Wider Curriculum Links
Report/ Instructional/ Persuasive	Interpreting information; language analysis; inferential comprehension	**History** Unit 14: Who were the Ancient Greeks?
Report	Making comparisons; expressing and justifying opinions	History Unit 19: What were the effects of Tudor exploration?
Persuasive	Understanding authorial intent; identifying fact and opinion; language analysis	**History** Unit 12: How did life change in our locality in Victorian times?
Recount	Close reading; interpreting information; expressing and justifying opinions	Geography Unit 24: Passport to the world
Explanation	Summarising and representing information; expressing and justifying opinions; asking questions	**Science** Unit 6F: How we see things
Report	Summarising information; language analysis; expressing and justifying opinions	Science Unit 6B: Micro-organisms
Report/ Explanation	Expressing and justifying opinions; close reading; asking questions	
Recount/ Report	Close reading; language analysis; expressing and justifying opinions	Design and Technology Unit 6C: Fairground
Explanation	Summarising information; using typography; inferential comprehension	
Instructional	Summarising information; expressing and justifying opinions; information retrieval	PSHE: Preparing to play an active role as citizens
Fun spread		
		ICT: Year 6 Schemes of work

WELCOME TO ANCIENT GREECE!

You've been whisked back in time to Ancient Greece. But how much do you know about the country you've arrived in? Test yourself with our fun quiz and, if you get stuck, see if you can find the answers in the Visitor's Guide opposite.

1. What is the Acropolis?
a) a night club in Sparta
b) a high, rocky hill in Athens city centre
c) a Greek taverna

2. What is the Parthenon?
a) a theatre
b) a famous racetrack
c) a temple to Athene

3. How would you describe a Greek temple?
a) a circular wooden building with a pointed roof
b) a rectangular, roofed building with tall, stone columns
c) a semi-circular building with rows of stone seats

4. Who is Zeus?
a) the King of Greece
b) a famous scientist
c) the ruler of the Greek gods

5. Where could you see a trireme?
a) in the harbour
b) at the theatre
c) at the market

6. What might an Ancient Greek offer you for lunch?
a) kebab and chips
b) bread, cheese, olives and figs
c) stuffed dormice in honey

7. Which is the Greeks' favourite form of entertainment?
a) theatre
b) cinema
c) bull fights

8. Which celebrities might you spot in Ancient Greece?
a) Cleopatra and Tutankhamun
b) Pythagoras and Archimedes
c) Caesar and Nero

9. How long do the Olympic Games last?
a) 5 days
b) 1 month
c) 4 years

10. Which would make a good souvenir of Ancient Greece?
a) a beautiful mosaic
b) a mummified cat
c) a piece of red and black pottery decorated with pictures

ATHENS – A VISITOR'S GUIDE

Climb to the top of the Acropolis and marvel at the views; hunt for souvenirs in the market place; admire the world-class architecture and enjoy lunch in olde-worlde taverns and bars. How about a day at the theatre or the games? Whatever your taste, there's plenty to enjoy in Athens and beyond.

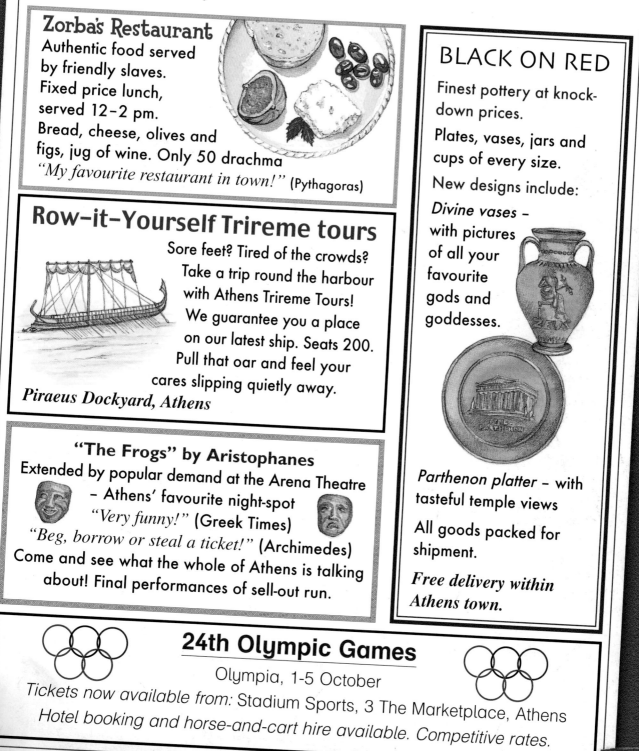

Zorba's Restaurant

Authentic food served by friendly slaves.
Fixed price lunch, served 12–2 pm.
Bread, cheese, olives and figs, jug of wine. Only 50 drachma
"My favourite restaurant in town!" (Pythagoras)

Row-it-Yourself Trireme tours

Sore feet? Tired of the crowds? Take a trip round the harbour with Athens Trireme Tours! We guarantee you a place on our latest ship. Seats 200. Pull that oar and feel your cares slipping quietly away.
Piraeus Dockyard, Athens

"The Frogs" by Aristophanes

Extended by popular demand at the Arena Theatre – Athens' favourite night-spot
"Very funny!" (Greek Times)
"Beg, borrow or steal a ticket!" (Archimedes)
Come and see what the whole of Athens is talking about! Final performances of sell-out run.

BLACK ON RED

Finest pottery at knock-down prices.

Plates, vases, jars and cups of every size.

New designs include:

Divine vases – with pictures of all your favourite gods and goddesses.

Parthenon platter – with tasteful temple views

All goods packed for shipment.

Free delivery within Athens town.

24th Olympic Games

Olympia, 1-5 October
Tickets now available from: Stadium Sports, 3 The Marketplace, Athens
Hotel booking and horse-and-cart hire available. Competitive rates.

In search of El Dorado

In 1595, Sir Walter Raleigh set sail from England on an expedition. He was looking for the legendary city of El Dorado, which he believed was in South America. Although El Dorado was never found, Raleigh and his crew did return to England with many riches, and stories of 'far off' places.

Life on board a Tudor galleon was dangerous and difficult. This inventory shows some of the things the sailors would have taken with them on their journey.

Navigation aids

The ship's pilot had to guide the ship across the oceans using only simple equipment and the stars.

o   magnetic compasses
o   traverse board – a pegboard with strings attached. This was used to record the journey so sailors could retrace their route
o   sundials and hour glasses
o   charts, tide-tables and pilots' books, containing information on coastlines, winds, dangerous reefs and tides
o   sounding lead – a lead weight on a rope which had a hollow end containing sticky animal fat which picked up sand from the seabed. This showed the pilot how deep the sea was.

Weapons

Trading ships were less heavily armed than warships, but they still carried weapons for defence against attack by pirates.

o   cannons
o   iron, stone and lead shot
o   gunpowder
o   handguns
o   carved wooden linstocks for lighting gunpowder
o   pikes, swords, bills and daggers for fighting pirate invaders
o   wooden bows and arrows made from goose or swan feathers

Medicine chest

This was used by the ship's barber-surgeon. He trimmed hair and beards, healed wounds and performed operations – including amputations!

O drug flask
O jars of herbal ointment
O syringes
O metal bleeding bowl
O barber's bowl
O mallets for knocking out patients before operations
O velvet caps worn by barber-surgeon
O bandages soaked in herbal lotions

Food supplies

The cooper looked after the wooden casks that contained food and drink. Most of the meat and fish was salted or smoked to stop it going bad.

O bacon, beef, pork, lamb, venison and fish
O biscuits
O damsons and plums
O water

Cooking and tableware

The cook and his assistants worked in the ship's galley, preparing meals.

O pewter and wooden plates
O knives and spoons
O leather and wooden flagons
O pepper mills
O pots and cauldrons for cooking
O leather water buckets for putting out fires
O candlesticks
O bellows
O wood for fuel to cook with

Entertainment

Sailors entertained themselves with gambling and board games. Musical instruments may also have helped to keep sailors in rhythm when pulling on sail ropes.

O dice and dominoes
O backgammon
O pipes and fiddles

Bathroom kits

Officers kept these with their personal belongings.

O folding manicure kit
O combs for getting rid of lice in hair
O spice-filled pomanders to hide bad smells
O bone scoops for cleaning out ears

Clothing repairs

The crew were responsible for keeping their own clothes in good repair.

O leather shoes
O ribbons and threads
O buttons, pins and thimbles
O weaving loom

DOMBEY & SON PROPERTY AGENTS

25 Wellington Gardens, Charlton
Just 5 miles south-east of the City of London

TO RENT: 12/6d per week

A newly-built two-storey terraced villa in excellent decorative order. Situated in a favoured locality within easy walking of local shops, parks and railway station with fast, efficient trains to the City, just five miles distant. The property boasts three bedrooms, two principal rooms, kitchen and scullery, and enjoys the unusual luxury of a plumbed-in bathroom. Offers attractive garden to rear. Must be viewed.

Front door to:

Entrance hall: Stairs to first floor, steep stairs to coal cellar, doors off.

Front parlour: 16'9" x 15'2"
Impress your visitors with this well-appointed room. Front aspect with bay window, marble fireplace with tile surround, easy-sweep wooden flooring, decorative ceiling plasterwork, picture rails for family portraits, full pipework to ornamental gas lamps, wood-panelled double doors to:

Dining room: 15'10" x 15'2"
A practical room for family use. Rear aspect with garden views, sash window for healthy ventilation, feature fireplace with easy-to-clean hearth, solid wooden flooring, decorative ceiling plasterwork, picture rails, gas piping, panelled door.

Kitchen: 14'2" x 13'3"
A clean, practical room for the lady of the house. Coal-fired range in excellent working order with back boiler and mantelpiece above, built-in dresser offers useful storage with drawers, cupboards and shelving, cool larder with marble shelf, built-in cupboard, sash window, gas piping, easy-clean linoleum flooring, panelled door to:

Scullery: 6'2" x 11'6"
Ease those washday blues with fully functioning washing copper, ceramic sink with tap, practical tiled floor, glazed door leading to rear garden.

Stairs lead to:

First floor landing:
Built-in cupboard for household linen, wooden flooring, dado rail, doors off.

Master bedroom: 15'5" x 14'8"
A spacious room offering quiet comfort. Front aspect via bay window, feature fireplace, easy-sweep wooden flooring, decorative plasterwork, picture rail, panelled door.

Bedroom 2: 10'10" x 10'1"
Roomy family accommodation. Rear aspect with garden views, sash window, built-in cupboard, cosy fireplace, picture rail, stained wooden flooring, panelled door.

Bedroom 3: 9'11" x 8'5"
Snug bedroom with front aspect, sash window, easy-clean fireplace, stained wooden flooring, panelled door.

Bathroom: 7'4" x 5'11"
Enjoy the luxury and privacy of your own bathroom with a plumbed-in cast-iron bathtub, frosted-glass window, wipe-down linoleum flooring, panelled door.

Outside:

Water closet:
Well-ventilated water closet with china bowl and cistern and warm wooden seat, connected to city sewerage system.

Back garden: Approx. 65' long
Charming garden laid to lawn with flowerbeds, gravelled pathway leading to small, productive vegetable patch and hen-coop.

Front garden: Approx. 12' long
Decorative tiled pathway, coal-hole leading to good-sized cellar.

TUESDAY MORNING

Beloved

I can't tell you where I am except that it's another country — I am a secret agent after all — but I promised to drop you a line every day, and here is the first. My mission is to track down a man known only as W, and follow him wherever he goes. I know nothing about him, or what he's done. All I have is an Identikit picture of him so that I will recognise him. In order not to stand out from the crowd, I have disguised myself as an ordinary working man of this country. It's difficult to recognise me in my little black beret, string of onions over my shoulder and accordion under my arm!

Will write again tomorrow.
Poochy X

WEDNESDAY EVENING

Sweetheart

So much happened after I wrote yesterday. I was sitting in a street cafe when W strolled by. He was the spitting image of my Identikit picture, so I had no doubt it was him. I jumped up and followed him to the railway station, where he bought a train ticket. I asked the ticket seller what W's destination was, and I bought a ticket for the same place. I found a seat at the other end of W's carriage, but held a newspaper up over my face throughout the journey so he wouldn't see me.

This is a very flat country, full of canals. I'm kept awake at night by a strange creaking sound. I have bought some local footwear which is really making my feet hurt, but I must wear it in order to blend in.

Don't forget to feed the fish.
Poochy X

Dearest

Shortly after we reached W's destination I lost him, but then he appeared again — handcuffed to another man! Obviously the other man was a policeman and he'd arrested W. It was tempting to introduce myself, but I held back. My job is to follow W, nothing more. So I followed him and the policeman in a cab to the airport, where they bought plane tickets. I found out which country they were headed for, and bought a ticket to the same place.

When we landed, I followed the policeman and his prisoner to what I imagine is a police station. It stands near a great ruined arena where I'm told gladiators used to fight and prisoners were set upon by lions. As I was lurking by the police station trying to decide what to do next, W suddenly came out — alone. He had escaped! What a cunning man he must be. I bought an ice-cream and a stuffed lion from a street vendor so that I would look like a tourist, and once again set off after the villain.

Love and kisses
Poochy X

FRIDAY EVENING

Darling

Well, we're certainly getting about. I don't know what he's up to, but W has once again led me to another country. I am typing this while W makes a phone call in a nearby park. I have bought a pair of castanets and a matador's hat, so that he'll think I belong here if he sees me. I have put the hat on over my beret, as I have become very fond of that little thing.

More tomorrow.
Poochy X

SATURDAY MIDNIGHT

Precious

I am in the country I started out in, to which the clever W has led me back. I write this by the light of the moon through the bars of my cell. Yes, my cell. I have been arrested — by W himself! He wasn't the person I was supposed to follow after all, but an Interpol agent. And the man I saw him handcuffed to the other day wasn't a policeman, but a prisoner W had been asked to escort to the city with the ancient arena.

W says he's been aware of me following him all the time. He knew I was up to no good, he tells me, because nobody wears a beret, a matador's hat, clogs, and carries a string of onions, an accordion and a stuffed lion all at once. Well, how was I to know?

Will you come and bail me out please? It's very boring here. There isn't even much to look at from my window — just a very tall tower that reminds me of Blackpool! See you soon. I hope.

Your very sad Poochy
XXX

EXTRAORDINARY ECLIPSES

Eclipses have fascinated us for thousands of years with their strange and eerie beauty. But why do these extraordinary events occur?

An eclipse is the darkening of a planet or moon. This happens when the shadow of one planet or moon falls onto another. There are two types of eclipse: a solar eclipse, which is an eclipse of the Sun, and a lunar eclipse, which is an eclipse of the Moon. They both occur when the Sun, Moon and Earth are in line with one another.

SOLAR ECLIPSE

An eclipse of the Sun occurs when the Moon lies between the Sun and the Earth. The Moon is just large enough to 'cover' the Sun, blocking its light, and casting a dark shadow on part of the Earth's surface. The shadow sweeps across the Earth as the Moon continues in its orbit.

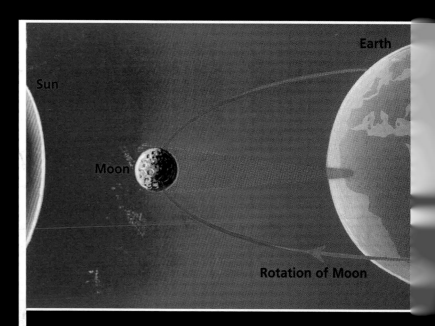

During a solar eclipse, the Moon blocks the light from the Sun

A halo of gases can be seen around the Sun during an eclipse. This is called the corona

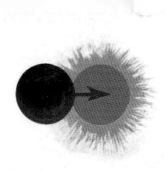

The Moon begins to move across the Sun

A minute or two later, the Moon blots out the Sun. All that can be seen is the Sun's corona

The Moon moves on, and the Sun reappears

LUNAR ECLIPSE

When the Earth lies between the Sun and the Moon, it blocks light from the Sun and casts a shadow on the Moon. This shadow moves slowly across the Moon's surface.

During a lunar eclipse, the moon darkens to a reddish colour

ANCIENT BELIEFS

For people who lived a long time ago, eclipses were very frightening. The ancient Chinese believed that a dragon in the sky was swallowing the Sun or Moon. In ancient Rome, an eclipse was a bad omen, a sign that something dreadful was about to happen. Ancient Greek scientists explained eclipses after recording the movement of the planets, moons and stars. From about 600 BC they were able to predict when the next eclipse

DID YOU KNOW?

- A solar eclipse can last up to seven minutes.
- A lunar eclipse can last for more than an hour.
- The last solar eclipse visible from the UK occurred on 11 August, 1999. Unfortunately, the sky was cloudy, which meant that in most areas the eclipse could not be seen clearly.
- The word 'eclipse' comes from a Greek word 'ekleipsis', which means 'failure to appear'.

Amazing microbes

What are the commonest living things on Earth? Are they human beings, insects, fish or trees? No — the most numerous living things are all around us, but they are so small we cannot see them! Micro-organisms (microbes for short) far outnumber all other forms of life. There are more microbes in your body (about 100 000 billion) than there are people in the whole world (about 6 billion).

Viruses

A microbe is any living thing that is too small to see with the naked eye. There are many different types, including bacteria, protozoa, and some kinds of fungi and algae. Viruses are sometimes called microbes too, though they are not strictly alive because they cannot reproduce unless they infect living cells.

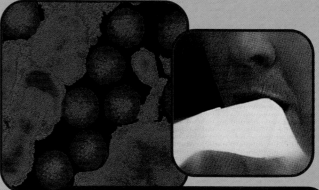

The cold virus is so small that billions of them can fit on a pinhead. It spreads by making you sneeze. A single sneeze ejects billions of virus particles into the air at more than 60 miles per hour!

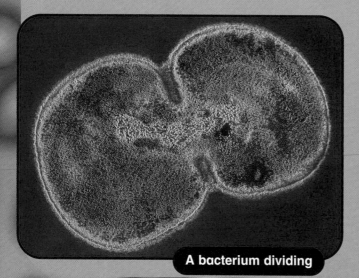

A bacterium dividing

Bacteria

Micro-organisms are rapid breeders. A bacterium, for example, reproduces by splitting in two, making a pair of identical clones. In the right conditions, bacteria divide every twenty minutes. In theory, a single bacterium could produce over a million offspring in just seven hours.

Germs

Many microbes cause disease by infecting and reproducing on or in our bodies. We often describe these microbes as germs or bugs. Athlete's foot, for example, is a skin infection caused by a microscopic fungus.

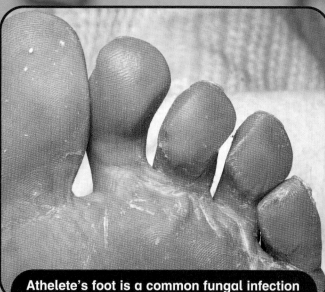

Athelete's foot is a common fungal infection of the feet. Washing feet daily and drying them carefully can help prevent infection

Rats

Plague

In the Middle Ages, the Plague swept through Europe, killing more than half the population. People believed that the disease was spread by 'bad air' or 'evil spirits'. In fact, it was caused by bacteria carried by fleas from infected rats to people. There are still occasional outbreaks of plague around the world today.

'Friendly' bacteria

Not all micro-organisms are harmful. Some are very useful. 'Friendly' bacteria in our intestines help us digest food. Other bacteria change milk into yoghurt and cheese. Yeasts

Cat flea

are microscopic fungi that change sugar into alcohol in beer and wine, and make bread rise before it is baked in the oven.

A sleepy story...

One third of your life will be spent in the dreamy world of sleep. We need sleep to live, just like we food and water. But why?

Sleeping to live

Although it may seem like you are not doing very much while you are sleeping, your body and brain are actually working quite hard. Sleep helps your body to grow and to stay healthy. It rests the muscles and allows the body to store energy for when you are awake. It also helps you to fight illness.

While you are sleeping, your brain makes sense of everything you have learned during the day. Sometimes you dream. You might even walk and talk in your sleep! If you don't get enough sleep, it becomes harder to concentrate and remember things.

Sweet dreams

Why do we dream? No one really knows. Many dreams are based on things that have happened in our lives. The things that are important to us – family, friends, sports, school work – can appear again and again in our dreams, sometimes in bizarre situations! Dreams can also be about fears, wishes and hopes. The brain can be so lively during a dream that you may feel as if you are running or shouting, or that you are cold or hungry.

The 'Sleep Cycle'

Stage one:
Your eyes close, your muscles relax, your heartbeat slows down and your breathing becomes even and steady. You are aware of faint sounds around you. This stage usually lasts 5 to 10 minutes.

Stage two:
For the next 15 to 30 minutes, you are asleep, but only just. If someone gave you a nudge, or your dog put its cold nose on your arm, you would quickly wake up.

Stage three:
Next, you spend a few minutes in a fairly deep sleep.

Stage four:
Now comes the deepest sleep stage, lasting from 30 to 40 minutes. Your body is still – there's no tossing and turning – and your breathing is deep and regular. It's difficult to wake someone up during this stage.

Stage five:
You change position. You go into a lighter sleep. And then you begin Rapid Eye Movement (REM) sleep. During REM, your eyes dart backwards and forwards beneath your closed eyelids. Your brain is working, just as it is when you're awake. This is the time when you dream! REM sleep lasts from 20 to 30 minutes.

All these stages together are called the 'sleep cycle.' One sleep cycle lasts from 90 to 100 minutes. After the first complete cycle the body usually returns to stage two sleep, and this cycle is repeated several times a night.

So as you get into bed tonight with droopy eyelids, just think about all the hard work your body and brain are about to do. Sweet dreams!

All Aboard the Eye

The London Eye

Today, I went on the London Eye with my mum and dad. It was amazing. We were in a passenger capsule which was completely enclosed, with glass walls and roof. As the wheel went round, really slowly, we had these fantastic views all over London.

I was really interested in the Eye, so I decided to find out more about it. It was built on the South Bank of the River Thames in 1999, to celebrate the Millennium. The wheel represents the turning of the century. Lots of people had ideas for a Millennium project but two architects, David Marks and Julia Barfield, thought of the Eye. It is the largest observation wheel ever built. It is 135 metres high, which makes it the fourth tallest structure in London. From the top of the wheel, you can see for over 40 km in all directions.

The Eye never stops moving. Passengers get on and off the capsules as they pass slowly by. It takes 30 minutes to go right round. We could walk around in our capsule, which held 25 people. There were seats in the middle, and some people sat on them to begin with because they were a bit scared of heights. But they soon got used to it because the capsules do not sway around like cars on a Ferris wheel, and there is a solid floor under your feet. The capsules are on the outside rim of the wheel so there is nothing to block the view.

A capsule

From our passenger capsule, we could see north, south, east and west as the Eye turned. I saw St Paul's Cathedral, the Houses of Parliament, the Tower of London, the British Telecom Tower and lots of other buildings. People were taking photographs from the capsule. Most people were really excited by the experience. They were pointing out what they could see in the different directions.

I will certainly go on the Eye again if I get the chance.

Eye Facts

The Eye was designed to be a bit like a giant bicycle wheel. It has a central hub and spindle which is connected to the outer and inner rims by 80 cable spokes. The spindle holds the wheel in place and the hub turns it round the spindle.

- The spindle is 23 metres tall, about the height of a church spire.
- The spindle and hub weigh 330 tonnes, which is heavier than Big Ben!
- 1700 tonnes of steel were used to build the Eye, which makes it heavier than 250 double-decker buses or 280 African elephants!
- The hub and spindle are supported by two 60-metre-high columns and secured to the ground by six huge cables. What makes the Eye really unusual is that it is supported from one side only.
- It took over a week to lift the Eye from a horizontal to a vertical position.

LIVING IN SPACE

Have you ever dreamed of living in space? Since the end of the 1950s, scientists have been making such dreams come true for many astronauts.

<<< ZERO GRAVITY >>>

Living in space is not easy. In space there is no gravity, and this 'zero gravity' is one of the biggest challenges for astronauts. On Earth, if you lifted your bicycle off the ground, you would notice the pull of gravity. Your bike would feel heavy and eventually you would have to put it down, and it would stay where you put it. However in space things are weightless. You would easily be able to lift your bike, but it wouldn't stay where you left it. It would float around the spacecraft and might even hit you on the head!

<<< HOLD TIGHT! >>>

Scientists have tried to make living in space easier. Guide lines are hung inside the spacecraft so that astronauts have something to hold on to. To make standing on the floor of the cabin easier, there are footholds attached to the floor. In order to make sure the crew is safe, equipment is strapped to the wall to stop it from floating around the spacecraft.

<<< FLOATING FOOD >>>

Many astronauts experience space sickness. Luckily, this only lasts for a few days, and scientists have found that travel sickness medicine usually does the trick. Eating and drinking can cause a few problems too. Imagine snacking on peanuts and lemonade when suddenly a peanut slips out of your hand. Do you chase after the floating peanuts first, or do you close off the clamp on the end of your straw to stop the lemonade from shooting out?

<<< COSMIC MEALS FOR ONE >>>

In the early days of space exploration, food was often freeze-dried or stuffed into tubes to prevent accidents. Today, space food is very much like the food we eat on Earth. Improvements in packaging mean that food stays fresh for longer and can be eaten before it floats away! Single-helping containers keep astronauts' food fresh and make it easy to eat. Several dishes are included on a tray that the astronaut attaches to their lap with a strap. The cutlery astronauts use is similar to ours. It also includes scissors for opening packages.

<<< IT'S GOOD TO TALK >>>

Long trips into space can be physically and mentally tiring for astronauts. In outer space, the bones and the muscles of the human body can weaken. Exercise can help solve some of these problems. Keeping in touch with friends and family on Earth is also good medicine for the mind!

What do you think?
Does it sound brilliant or like hard work?

ST. JOHN AMBULANCE

Caring for Life

St. John Ambulance is a First Aid, transport and care charity. Its volunteers are trained in First Aid and medical support. You often see them in black and white uniform at public events such as big sporting events, street carnivals, fairs and fêtes.

St. John Ambulance is a major youth organisation, as many of its volunteers are under the age of 18. They are trained to give First Aid in an emergency. Here are some of the things they learn:

Rinsing burns under cold water can help ease the pain

Scalds and burns

All burns, except the most severe, need to be cooled as quickly as possible. First rinse the burn in cold water until the pain begins to go away. If clothes are sticking to the burn, do not try to remove them, but do remove loose or wet clothes. Dress the burn with a clean, non-fluffy dressing. Do not rub the skin or put any ointments onto the burn. Bad scalds and burns may need medical attention from a doctor.

Chemical burns

Be careful that you do not get the chemical on yourself. Gently wash the chemical away, taking care not to rub or injure the skin. Find out what the chemical is so that you can tell the doctors later. Try to take off any clothing that had the chemical spilt on it, and throw away the water you have washed the burn with.

Clothes on fire

Stop the person running around in a panic as this makes the flames worse. Lay them down and put the flames out with water, or by wrapping them up in a large piece of material such as a rug or coat. Wrap the material tightly round their body to stop air getting to the flames. Never use materials that can catch fire or melt, such as nylon.

Choking

If someone gets something stuck in their throat and begins to choke, what do you do? If they cannot cough to get rid of the object, give them several hard slaps on the back between the shoulder blades. If possible, make them lean forward so that the object can fall out easily.

Clearing a blocked airway

The recovery position

An unconscious person lying on their back should be put into the recovery position. This prevents the tongue from blocking the throat. Kneel beside the person and open their airway by tilting the head backwards. The arm nearer to you should be placed at right-angles to the person's body, with the elbow bent and the palm of the hand facing upwards. Bring the other arm across the chest and hold the hand, palm outwards, against their cheek. Grasp the thigh that is further from you and pull the person's knee up, keeping their foot flat on the ground. Pull at the thigh to roll the person onto their side. Make adjustments to make sure that the airway is kept clear.

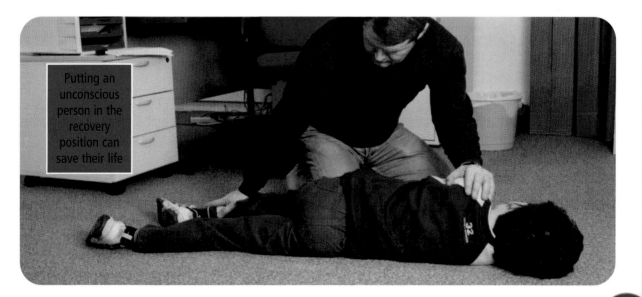

Putting an unconscious person in the recovery position can save their life

Are you amazing?

Are you a whiz at quizzes? To answer the following questions you'll need to look back through this amazing edition of *The Navigator*. If you've read the pages carefully you should have no trouble completing the quiz. If I'm feeling generous, I might give you some clues!

1. Where is the London Eye situated?

2. You are a sailor on a Tudor galleon and the captain orders you to clean out your ears. What tool would you use to do this?

3. Which language does the word 'eclipse' come from?

4. How does the secret agent disguise himself on Tuesday morning?

5. If a person is choking, where should you slap them?

Hint: They're green and live in ponds . .

6. While in Ancient Greece you decide to go to see a play by Aristophanes at the Arena Theatre in Athens. What is it called?

7. How many microbes are there in your body?

8. Victorian property agents Dombey & Son are showing you round 25 Wellington Gardens. Where would you find the well-ventilated water closet?

9. What does REM stand for?

10. You need an operation on your leg while at sea on a Tudor galleon. What would the barber-surgeon use from his medicine chest instead of anaesthetic?

Warning: This may hurt a bit!

11. What is the name for the halo of gases that can be seen around the sun during an eclipse?

12. What pets does the secret agent have at home?

13. In the Middle Ages, which insects carried the plague bacteria from infected rats to people?

14. What is the Acropolis?

Hint: It's not a nightclub in Sparta!

15. Name three landmarks that you can see from the London Eye.

16. The secret agent discovers the true identity of the man he has been following. Who is W?

17. What does putting an unconscious person in the recovery position prevent?

18. How fast are virus particles released into the air when you sneeze?

19. You have called upon the services of Dombey & Son property agents to help you find a house to rent in Victorian England. They suggest 25 Wellington Gardens, Charlton. How far is this outside the city of London?

20. What happens to an astronaut's bones and muscles in space?

Byte-Sized ICT

Welcome to Ancient Greece!

Greek art

Look at the Greek-style border pattern along the top and bottom of pages 4 and 5. Greeks typically used simple, repeated, symmetrical patterns on items such as pottery and for friezes on buildings. Try using an art program on your computer to create a Greek-style pattern and repeat it to make a border. Stick to Greek colours of black and reddish-orange.

If you like, you can also have a go at drawing a picture of Greek life or illustrating a Greek myth. Again, these were usually black on orange – so you will need to fill in the background of your picture, instead of leaving it white.

In search of El Dorado
Who was Sir Walter Raleigh?

How much do you know about Sir Walter Raleigh? Everyone seems to know his name and that he sailed to America on an expedition, but what about the finer details? When was he born? How and why did he become an explorer? What did he discover on his voyage? When and how did he die?

Research Sir Walter Raleigh's life, using whatever sources are available to you (books, CD-ROM, Internet). Then type up a short biographical fact-file of him using a word processor. Try setting out the questions or sub-headings in bold and the answers in ordinary type. You could use bullet points to make it clearer. Keep it in note form. You even may be able to copy and paste a picture of him into your fact-file.

Dombey & Son property agents
Online agents

These days, not only can you visit an estate agent or look in the newspaper to find a new home, but you can also search the web. Try finding out about property prices in your area by searching the Internet for a new home!

Most well-known estate agents have websites. Some even include photos or virtual tours of the houses. Try typing the name of an estate agent in your area (you can usually find these in any local newspaper) followed by .co.uk or .com.

A sleepy story...

Dream or nightmare?

Have you ever had an amazing dream or a horrible nightmare? Was it so vivid that you could recall all of it in the morning? Was it so weird that no one believed you?

Why not try to catch out your friends? Type three short summaries of dreams or nightmares. At least one of them should be entirely made-up, the others should be ones you have really dreamed. Can your friends guess which are true and which are false? Maybe your actual dreams are weirder than anything you could invent!

Living in space

Space special!

ICT: Unit 6a: Multimedia presentation

The theme of space has inspired so much research as well as so many films, books and pieces of music. Let space inspire you! Try creating a multimedia presentation about some aspects of space.

You could include some space-type sounds or music, perhaps linked by including a button on your screen. How about some space facts? You could even put in some animated diagrams or pictures. Remember to view your presentation yourself before presenting it to others. Check all your links work and that you are happy with it.

All Aboard the Eye

What to see, where to go

ICT: Unit 6d: Using the Internet

It's a great idea to use the web to look up famous tourist attractions, like the London Eye, before you make a trip there. You can find opening times, prices, how to get there, views of the attraction and often extra information for children or visiting schools.

Try locating the websites of some famous attractions in this country (perhaps within easy reach of your area) and compile the 'top three' websites. Look at how well laid-out each website is, how easy it is to navigate your way around, and how useful the information is. What features do you especially like about it? Does it make you want to go there?

Helpful hint!

Most well-known attractions use their name followed by .co.uk. If this doesn't work, try .com instead. If the name has several words in it, such as 'Tower of London' sometimes there are dashes in between the words, but no gaps.

Glossary

amputation	having a part of the body surgically removed
astronauts	people trained to operate and travel in a spacecraft
bellows	a device for pumping a stream of air
bizarre	very strange indeed
bleeding bowl	the bowl in which blood was caught when it was drawn off for medical reasons
capsule	the part of a spacecraft that holds the crew and the instruments
cooper	someone who makes and repairs wooden barrels
destination	the place or point to which you are going
eerie	strange and frightening
eject	throw out
flagons	large bottles or containers
gravity	the force that attracts objects to the centre of the Earth
hub	the centre of a wheel
legendary	very well-known
linstocks	poles with flammable rags on the ends for lighting cannons

manicure kit	tools for cutting and filing fingernails
mosaic	a pattern made from small pieces of coloured glass, stone or tiles
mummified	shrivelled and dried up like a mummy
pewter	a metal made from tin and lead used for making plates and mugs
represent	stand for or act on behalf of something or someone
scullery	a small kitchen at the back of the house used for washing up, etc.
spindle	a revolving rod or shaft in a machine, around which another part turns
terrace	a row of joined houses
trireme	a type of warship used in Ancient Greece
venison	the meat of a deer
ventilation	the circulation of air
washing copper	a large open-topped container made of copper or iron. A fire was lit under it and washing boiled in it

Index